35 WAYS TO GIVE YOURSELF A LITTLE TLC

TRANSFORMATIONAL **L**IFESTYLE **C**ARE

Tawawn Lowe

TLC PUBLISHING COMPANY

www.tawawn.com

35 Ways to Give Yourself A Little **TLC**
Transformational Lifestyle Care

Copyright @ 2020 by TLC Publishing Company

No part of this book may be reproduced or transmitted in any form or by any means, electronic or mechanical, including photocopying, recording or any information storage and retrieval system without the permission of the publisher except for brief quotations used in reviews, written specifically for inclusion in a newspaper or magazine.

This book is available for quantity discounts for bulk purchases.

Library of Congress Cataloging-in-Publication Data is available upon request.

ISBN: 978-1-64713-326-9

All rights reserved.
Printed in the United States of America

DISCLAIMER
Although you may find the affirmative expressions to be useful, the book is sold with the understanding that neither the co-authors nor TLC Publishing Company, are engaged in presenting any legal, relationship, financial, emotional, or health advice. The purpose of this book is to educate and entertain. The co-authors and publishers shall neither assume liability nor responsibility for anyone with respect to any loss or damage caused directly or indirectly by the information in the book.

Any person who is experiencing financial, anxiety, depression, health, mental health, or relationship issues should consult with a licensed therapist, advisor, licensed psychologist, or other qualified professional before commencing into anything described in this book. This book intends to provide you with the writers' insights and reflections on the four subjects in the book. All results will differ; however, our goal is to provide you with affirmative expressions to use as a practical approach to foster powerful change within your life.

35
Ways to Give Yourself A Little TLC

Transformational Lifestyle Care

TO: _____

FROM: _____

This book is dedicated to those individuals who struggle with putting themselves first, who are ignoring their own needs, and are not making self-care an important of their regiment for their overall well-being.

We hope this book encourages you to make yourself a priority, and give yourself permission to relax,
release and restore.

All you need is

A Little **TLC**!

TABLE OF CONTENTS

Introduction ix
1. Cut back or Ditch the Caffeine 1
2. Have a Cup of Chamomile Tea 2
3. Get A Good Night Sleep 3
4. Lose Yourself in A Good Book 4
5. Listen to Music 5
6. Try ASMR 6
7. Take Power Naps 7
8. Try Aroma Therapy 8
9. Warm Up 9
10. Cool Down 10
11. Get a Pet 11
12. Massage Therapy 12
13. Have a Glass of Wine 13
14. Quit Smoking 14
15. Have Some Dark Chocolate 15
16. Get a Hobby 16
17. Art Therapy 17
18. Go to a Spa or Wellness Retreat 18
19. Get a Change of Scenery 19
20. Change Your Perspective 20
21. Take Advantage of Brief Moments 21
22. Think and Visualize Calmness 22

23. Unplug 23
24. Yoga 24
25. Mindful Breathing 25
26. Meditation 26
27. Keep a Journal 27
28. Be Grateful 28
29. Take a Day Off 29
30. Get Some Fresh Air 30
31. Adult Coloring 31
32. Go for a Run 32
33. Declutter 33
34. Don't Give Up on Relaxation 34
35. Talk to Someone 35
About the Visionary of Everybody Needs A Little TLC 37

Introduction

How do you kick back, chill out and really relax? Or a better question might be do you take time out from the busyness of life to give yourself a little TLC.... transformational lifestyle care? I know these sound like simple questions, but the truth is most people do not know how to give themselves a little TLC needed to relax, and restore themselves. Not only do they not know how to give themselves a little TLC to make relaxing a critical part of their self-care/self-maintenance.

We live in a fast pace, and frantic world; and between life, and work demands, we are constantly on the go. Most people are on the hamster wheel day in, and day out working hard in their careers, parenting, running businesses, being a spouse, giving back in the community, and maintaining a social life. We live in a busy society, where operating on automatic pilot has become the norm. When our lives are on automatic pilot with no turn off, often time taking time for self, and giving ourselves the TLC needed becomes a blur. Running all day long can feel exhilarating and productive, but it eventually wears us down and takes a toll on our total well-being.

Turning off, giving yourself a little TLC, and being able to relax your mind, body and spirit from the day-to-day grind and craziness can be difficult. It is a big challenge for many, for a multitude of reasons. While turning off can be hard, it is necessary. Stress is an inevitable part of life, and learning how to disconnect, and relax is essential to your self-care and stress management practices. Whether it is releasing physical tension, getting a load off your mind, or restoring your emotional health, we all need to take time out to relax. Everybody needs a little TLC!

We all owe ourselves one hour a day of TLC for our self-maintenance. There are many of ways to relax, release and restore. It can be as simple as reading, exercising, coloring, mediation, or journaling. The bottom line is we all owe it to ourselves to take care of ourselves. To give ourselves that TLC needed to help with keeping our body, mind and spirit in harmony. One hour, 1/24 of your day. This is less than 5%.

We all are different in terms of mind, body, and spirit. We have different stressors and preferred ways of how we relax and reduce stress. Our common goal should be to make transformational lifestyle care a habit that contributes to our emotional, intellectual, mental, physical, and spiritual well-being.

In this book, we provide 35 simple, yet effective ways to relax your mind, body and spirit that are easy to work into your everyday life. Some of the recommendations will be new to you, something you might already know but do not practice, or require you to give up some things.

Everybody needs a little TLC!

Are you ready to start implementing simple, yet effective practices into your everyday routine? It is time to give yourself time to relax, release and restore? Make yourself a priority, and give yourself permission to slow down and take care of you. Everybody wants to live their best life, but your best life requires you to take time for you to relax, and definitely restore yourself.

35
Ways to Give Yourself A Little TLC

Transformational Lifestyle Care

IN ORDER TO give yourself a little TLC you first have to be intentional about yourself self-care. You have to make a conscious decision for develop a habit that consist of a little TLC. Give yourself permission to make your self-care a priority. A part of your personal success encompasses your ability to take care of yourself. Striving for greatness is good, and a big part of your greatness is taking care of you.

As you go through this book, I challenge you to try every one of the 35-ways listed. Learn more about what helps you to relax, release, and restore, remember, everybody needs a little TLC, you owe it yourself.

1

Cut back or Ditch the Caffeine

MANY OF US need that one – or four large cups of Starbucks or Dunkin Donuts coffee or energy drink to start the day, but too much caffeine can make you too high-strung. According to WebMD, drinking too much caffeine can trigger symptoms of anxiety, jitters, GI discomfort, change in heart rate, and disrupt sleep. Because caffeine is a stimulant drug design to keep you up and alert – the consumption of it makes it hard for the body to rest and relax. Because caffeine is like a drug, dropping the caffeine habit can be hard. If you can't totally give up caffeine, start reducing how much you intake a day. Cut back on the coffee, energy drinks, sodas, and other foods that are high in caffeine.

2

Have a Cup of Chamomile Tea

WHILE TOO MUCH caffeine from sources like coffee and tea can leave you wound up, a hot cup of chamomile tea has some calming and relaxing effects. Because of tea calming effects and warmth tea is being used to help people to fall asleep, relax, and calm down after a busy day. According to 2017 Llewellyn's Herbal Almanac, chamomile tea in particular has a calming effect on the nerves. The Herbal Almanac also recommends making a soothing balm out of chamomile, lavender, and almond oil. This balm can be massaged into aching muscles to relax your body as well as your mind.

3

Get A Good Night Sleep

WHAT BETTER WAY to relax than getting a good night sleep. Getting good sleep and establishing healthy sleep habits is very important to self-care/maintenance and achieving your optimal health. Establishing healthy sleep habits is the best way for you to get a better sleep, and make difference in your quality of life. To help you relax and develop healthy sleep habits consider implementing the following: 1) stick to a sleep schedule even on the weekends, 2) make your bedroom conducive for sleeping (60-69 degrees), free from noise that disturb your sleep (earplugs for the snoring hubby, or partner), blackout curtains, eye shades, white noise machine, or humidifiers are just a few suggestions.

4

Lose Yourself in A Good Book

"ESCAPISM" IN A literary context is often used to refer to people's tendency to read books, especially fiction, as a way of "escaping" from their day-to-day grind. Reading can be a wonderful (and healthy) escape from the stress of everyday life. Simply by opening a book, you allow yourself to be invited into a literary world that distracts you from your daily stressors. Reading can even relax your body by lowering your heart rate and easing the tension in your muscles. A 2009 study at the University of Sussex found that reading could reduce stress by up to 68%. So, grab a book where the subject or story captures your interest, and provide a space for your mind to relax.

5

Listen to Music

MUSIC CAN OFFER a healthy and therapeutic way to relax. The right music has an awesome way of transporting you into another space. Listening to relaxing music helps you to maintain emotional balance – at home, work, while traveling, and particularly while driving. Listening to deep relaxing music allows you to let go of worry, and escape into the pleasures of the imagination allowing you to have a calming effect.

6

Try ASMR

IF YOU WANT something a little different from music, try Autonomous Sensory Meridian Response or ASMR for short. ASMR videos are a very popular on streaming sites like YouTube right now. The videos feature some quiet sound like whispering or gentle tapping that help some people to feel more relax, and fall asleep.

7
Take Power Naps

IF YOU DID not get a good night's sleep, that does not mean that all hope is lost. According to a 2015 article published in The Huffington Post, getting a nap during the day after a poor night's sleep can do you wonders. Not only does a nap give the mind and body the rest that it may have missed, it also helps the body catch up on making feel-good chemicals that it makes while you sleep.

8

Try Aroma Therapy

CHAMOMILE IS NOT the only plant that can help to soothe your mind. Some smells have the ability to temporarily ease the stress of the day. Scents have the power to evoke emotions and memories instantly and can directly affect your body through your nervous system. Aromatherapy is a complementary and alternative medicine practice that taps into the healing power of scents from essential oils extracted from plants in or order to balance your mind, body and spirit. A 2017 Huffington Post article by Dr. Marlynn Wei recommends combatting stress with essential oils made from Lavender, Lemon, Bergamot, Ylang Ylang, Clary Sage, and Jasmine.

9
Warm Up

HEAT RELAXES MUSCLES, banishes tightness and tension and allows the mind and body to relax. A 2017 Psychology Today article by Dr. Mithu Storoni wrote about studies conducted over the last few years that have found that warming our bodies may help to warm out hearts. This warmth can come from taking a hot bath or shower, holding someone you love, or even holding a cup of coffee.

10

Cool Down

ICE MIGHT NOT feel as relaxing as heat but according to Men's Journal, it actually does a better job of relaxing muscles and speeding up recovery. There is a hidden link between relaxation and pain relief. When you relieve pain, the brain sends the body a signal letting it know its okay to relax and release the stress and anxiety from the pain.

11

Get a Pet

PETS ARE NOT only cute; they also are good for stress relief. If you do not have a pet already, think twice about getting one. Affection does not have to be exchanged between people to help you to relax. According to a 2017 article in Time Magazine, studies have shown that people who own pets tend to have lower stress levels and blood pressure, helps their bodies release relaxation hormone, and other physical health benefits.

12

Massage Therapy

MASSAGE THERAPY IS a proven way to unwind, relax, release and restore. They relax the over-active minds, provides euphoric effects, have anti-depressive benefits, reduces stress hormones and anti-inflammatory effects, and increases serotonin and dopamine levels (which makes us happy). The effects of massages are well known that the number of American receiving massages has spike. In 2018, 4 of 10 Americans visited massage therapists according to study by the American Massage Therapy Association. Massage therapy relaxes and relieves stress through a number of ways, aside from the massage itself. The relaxing environment, use of aromatherapy, which helps to calm the mind, body and spirit, and the healing hands, is part of the process.

13

Have a Glass of Wine

GRAB YOUR FAVORITE Bordeaux glass, favorite Merlot or Cabernet and enjoy a glass of wine. A 2012 Psychology Today article by Dr. Adi Jaffe reports that studies have found that people who engage in moderate alcohol consumption have healthier stress levels than those who do not. Drinking red wine every night can help you sleep better and live longer (per google). A new study says that wine is good for you in multiply ways. Doctor say that alcohol in moderation help you relax

14

Quit Smoking

AN INTERESTING CASE of drugs that some of us use to relax is nicotine. This common drug found in tobacco products helps us to relax mentally – for a very short time – but has the opposite effect on our bodies. In the end, the tensing effect that nicotine has on our bodies is quantifiably more significant – and longer lasting ~ than the calming effect that it has on our minds.

15

Have Some Dark Chocolate

ONE MOOD ENHANCING concoction that you do not need to be afraid of is dark chocolate. Dark chocolate has been making people feel better for ages. A 2009 article by WebMD reported on research that showed that individuals who regularly ate dark an average-sized bar of dark chocolate each day for two weeks had lower levels of key stress hormones in their bodies. Eating one piece of dark chocolate may help you relax in the moment but eating one piece per day might have you feeling more relaxed all the time.

16

Get a Hobby

JUST THE ACT of having a hobby can make you feel more balanced in your lifestyle. Sometimes, with all of life's responsibilities, we forget that we need and deserve 'down time' and self-care. Taking even a few minutes on a regular basis to devote to a hobby can give you more of what you need in this area. In addition, with art therapy or adult coloring, you have the additional benefit of being left with something beautiful (or at least interesting) to show for it.

17

Art Therapy

ONE OF THE reasons that clinical art therapy is effective is that the act of drawing and creating art can help you relieve stress. Art therapy is a way of relieving stress and expressing emotion through art.

18

Go to a Spa or Wellness Retreat

ANOTHER STEP TOWARD leading a more mindful and meditative life can be to learn what relaxes you. Many cities have spas where you can go for a day to experience things like aromatherapy or massage. Many fitness centers, public gyms, or universities will have classes on relaxing activities like yoga. If you have the time and the means, a 2018 report by Bloomberg announced that the "wellness tourism" industry is booming and taking a vacation to a wellness resort can help to reset your stress levels and teach you some lasting tools.

19

Get a Change of Scenery

ACCORDING TO LIFEHACK.COM, you do not need to take a vacation, or even a day off away from your problems to relax a little, any change of scenery will do. Even if you are still working, bring it into the next room and see if you do not feel a little better.

20

Change Your Perspective

You may be able to downplay your stress and relax a little while staying productive by changing your perspective on your stress. Dr. Barbara Markway wrote in a 2013 Psychology Today article that "thanking our minds" for stress helps it to go away. This tactic involves reminding our stressful mind that we are in control of the situation.

21

Take Advantage of Brief Moments

A 2017 ARTICLE published in The Huffington Post suggests that even when we cannot make room for space between tasks, we can sometimes make room for space between thoughts. Instead of trying to fill every moment of the day, try to take advantage of those few minutes before a meeting, or after phone call.

22

Think and Visualize Calmness

As a man or woman thinketh, so he/she is - you can become what you think and believe. According to the Mayo Clinic, imagining visual images and calm thoughts is enough to help some people to relax. It only takes a moment and you can do it anywhere.

23
Unplug

SOMETIMES YOU HAVE to unplug to reconnect. Disconnect and unplug from all the ways you interact with others: silence your phone, turn off the computer, disconnect from all social media, and find a quiet space to relax your mind, your body and spirit. Relaxing your mind and turn the brain semi-off is hard. Unplugging allows you to step away from the stimulants, the noise, interaction and connection and relax.

24
Yoga

TRADITIONALLY, YOGA COMPRISED of the physical practice and breathing exercises – as well as other elements of a more religious or philosophical nature. These days many people practice the physical exercises that you usually think of when you come across the word "yoga" to reap its physical benefits, and many people practice the breathing aspect of yoga to reap its mental health benefits. The greatest benefit is found when both of these aspects of yoga are practiced together. A meta-analysis published in The Journal of Alternative and Complimentary Medicine in 2009 found that a regimen including mindful breathing and yoga practice helped to reduce stress in participants.

25

Mindful Breathing

MINDFUL BREATHING HELPS to control stress by allowing you to control an aspect of your biology that is often controlled by the subconscious. The physical practice of yoga helps your mental health by focusing your attention on your bodies rather than what is going on around you. It can also help you work out those knots that your bodies can accumulate during a stressful day.

26

Meditation

DR. ROBERT ORNSTEIN wrote in his 2008 book "Meditation and Modern Psychology" that the "mantras" ~ words repeated to one's self or out loud, often in a low hum – that are often associated with meditation can have religious meaning to religious practitioners but that they serve the practical purpose of "turning off awareness." "Turning off awareness" is a good way to temporarily escape from the day and reset your stress levels. In mindful breathing, it is done by focusing on the breath but in meditation, it is often done with a mantra. Repeating a mantra helps to keep the mind focused on the repetition of the word rather than on the stresses of the day. Your mantra could be one of the classic mantras associated with religious meditation, or it could be any other arbitrary or made up word.

27

Keep a Journal

WRITING IN YOUR journal is a healthy and therapeutic way to relax and distress. Whether journaling daily, weekly, monthly, or whenever needed, journaling is healthy a way to release negative feelings and thoughts, and handle stress and anxiety. Dr. James Pennebaker wrote in his 2003 book "Writing to Heal" that taking an event and our feelings about it and expressing them in language makes them easier for us to understand and process. Journaling can be coupled with drinking a hot cup of tea, mediation, listening to good music, the burning of essentials oils, or taking a day off.

28

Be Grateful

LONG AGO JEWISH thinkers knew that gratitude for what you have helped you to be more grateful and less worried about what you need or want. It has taken until fairly recently for scientists to suggest that taking the time to be grateful for things helps us to become more positive people. Dr. Alex Korb wrote in Psychology Today in 2012 that people who keep a journal of their gratitude had decreased symptoms of anxiety and depression. Having a divine connection with something greater than ourselves reminds us to be grateful for what we have because it takes little to survive and only slightly more to be happy. Practicing present moment gratitude each day, and allow yourself to feel grateful for what you do have. Living in the moment of gratitude causes a physical, emotional and spiritual calmness that bring forth peace (mental relaxation).

29

Take a Day Off

MOST RELIGIOUS TRADITIONS also recommend taking a day off each week. While this is often framed in terms of respecting that in the creation story God took one day off after taking six days to create the universe, it should also remind us that – in the words of the old Blues song – "every creature needs some rest."

In some conservative religious traditions taking a day off means that you do not shop, cook, or even turn on lights. If you are taking a day off for your health more than for your good, however, just put off things that you have to do in favor of things that you want to do even if they require work, like gardening.

30

Get Some Fresh Air

A STUDY CONDUCTED in 2007 and later published in The Journal of Social Issues tested individuals' moods before and after they spent time in a city and in a forest. The study found that those that spent time in a forest had better moods than those in the city.

If you work or live in the city but know that you prefer other environments, your mental health should be a good reason to make it out to the country or woods, or even just a nature park, as often as possible.

Even if you enjoy the city, sometimes its stresses – social and environmental – can get to you. Consider taking a trip to some more fresh air the next time that you get the opportunity. It may help enhance your mood, and the city will still be there when you get back.

31

Adult Coloring

COLORING BOOKS ARE no longer just for children. In fact, coloring for adults is the craze these days – and for good reason. Adults are discovering that coloring has many benefits that contribute to developing a calming mind, distressing, reducing anxiety and contributing to their overall mental and emotional well-being.

32

Go for a Run

FRESH AIR IS great, but any time outside is important. A 2012 study of recreational runners in urban Budapest found that the runners' moods were improved after their run even though they were running in the city as opposed to through a forest like the individuals in the above study.

The runners in this study were already recreational runners rather than random participants, so it could be that running improved their mood not because they were spending time outside but because they enjoyed running. In that case, you might as well give running a shot. Maybe it is your stress relief too.

33

Declutter

HAVE YOU EVER felt like a mess spiritual, mentally and emotionally? Sometimes we have to declutter our mind to bring it, our body and spirit into alignment. To declutter your mind, you have to become intentional on where you place your attention, and how you spend your time and energy. Here are a few suggestions on how to declutter your mind: Journal, exercise, let go of negative thoughts and feelings, get counseling, prayer/mediation, and laugh, unplug, be honest about your feelings, live in the present, and give your worries to God, priorities your commitments. These are just a few things to help you let go of something, or better handle issues and situations in your life.

34

Don't Give Up on Relaxation

IF NONE OF the tips so far has worked for you, keep trying them. A 2015 article published in Lifehack reminds us that sometimes our minds and bodies cannot just calm down, they need to learn to be calm.

If you are used to being busy, you might not be able to just sit down and feel your feet on the floor, at least not for very long. Just like anything else, it might take practice. Knowing that you are working toward learning to relax might be a bit relaxing in itself.

35

Talk to Someone

IF YOU REALLY cannot relax, if nothing in this book has worked for you and you feel like you just cannot relax, or always stressed, you might need more help.

Consider talking to a health care provider about anxiety.

Many people do not believe it is necessary to talk with a professional about their inability to relax, or make themselves a priority to take time out for relaxation. Talking to a doctor or mental health specialist about your inability to relax can help you learn to make yourself a priority, how to practice self-care, and give yourself that transformational lifestyle care you need.

Final Thoughts....

Everybody needs a little TLC. We all need to practice self-care/maintenance in the form of relaxations, and all of us have different ways of relaxing. The purpose of providing yourself a little TLC in the form of relaxation is to provide your body, mind and spirit to relax, release and restore. These three key elements are essential to your overall well-being. I hope that you have tried one, or more of the suggestions within the book; and that it has helped you implementing more practice of self-care/maintenance within your life.

Remember you owe it to yourselves to relax, release and restore.

Tawawn Lowe

About the Visionary of Everybody Needs A Little TLC

Tawawn is the CEO of TLConsultancy, LLC, founder of the Women Walking in their Own Shoes™ Movement, an **Amazon #1 bestselling author**, certified life coach, speaker, and creator of ***the Achieve Big Now Academy*™**.

TLConsultancy is a woman-and minority-owned multifaceted company based in Maryland that provides consulting and mentorship to individuals; learning/leadership-based solutions for organizations, and the umbrella for the Women Walking in Their Own Shoes™ Movement. Tawawn has blended her formal education, various certifications, and over 25+ years of professional experience to assist **organization with leadership development; and individuals with maximizing their full potential to achieve success.**

Tawawn's Why… For more than half her life, Tawawn believed her life had no real purpose. She turned someone else's limited belief about her potential into a self-fulfilling prophecy, making it true. She secretly lived an unhappy and unfilled life because she believed success could not be a part of her story. After having an "aha moment", she realized she had given away her power. This revelation led to her taking full charge of her own destiny, and to envision a different future for her life.

In October 2012, TLE expanded their mission and launched the Movement - Women ***Walking in their Own Shoes*** (WWITOS) ™. The Movement is a clarion call to action to women globally to say, "YES", giving themselves permission to become their best selves, create their best lives, and achieve success on their own terms (walk in their own shoes).

Tawawn is here to serve you. Her goal is simple, to help others take charge of their destiny, transform visions into results, and achieve success on their own terms. A part of taking charge of destiny is practicing self-care and self-maintenance. She understands that you can't be your best self, or create your best life if you don't take care of you.

Everybody Needs A Little TLC!

For additional information on TLC Publishing Company or TLConsultancy, please visit Tawawn on the web at

www.tawawn.com

Follow Us on Social Media

Tawawn
TL_Consultancy and tlc_boxes
TL_Consultancy

www.ingramcontent.com/pod-product-compliance
Lightning Source LLC
LaVergne TN
LVHW081525060526
838200LV00044B/2008